Appletree Guides

THE

IRISH

LANDSCAPE

JAMES BRINDLEY

GW00514689

First published and printed in 1989 by
The Appletree Press Ltd
7 James Street South
Belfast BT2 8DL

Photographs: Bord Failte, the author

The publisher gratefully acknowledges the
assistance of Mary Mallon in the preparation of
this book.

**British Library Cataloguing in
Publication Data**
A catalogue record for this book is available
from the British Library.

ISBN 0 86281 310 7

9 8 7 6 5 4 3 2

Contents

Introduction

The Irish landscape is a complex of many factors, some of which range far back in time while others are still at work today, yet all are interesting, and a knowledge of how they operate will add to the enjoyment of many a familiar scene. Ireland's regional characteristics are very distinctive: Kerry and Antrim, Clare and Dublin, Donegal and Wexford; each has its own pleasant type of scenery. More impressive than anything else, however, are the striking contrasts on a local scale: the little lakes tucked away among Cavan's drumlins, the broad plains and rugged mountains of the west, the crowded islands and sweeping hills around Clew Bay. Ireland's native landscape artists: Hone, O'Connor, Henry and Wilks, have captured the moods of this land very sensitively, yet their impressions are different indeed, for the Irish scene can vary enormously in storm and in sunshine, in winter and in summer.

The cause of its diversity is not far to seek. An island exposed on the Atlantic seaboard, its coastline is rugged to an unusual degree. The land itself is rich and green, moistened by the prevailing south-westerlies and mellowed by the Gulf Stream which warms its shores. Though they embrace no great extremes its climatic vagaries may be disconcerting in the suddenness with which they change its character, and underlying all is the influence of its rock formations and of its surface development which gives to each Irish panorama a unique aspect.

The land is old. Its most ancient rock formations date back a thousand million years and have undergone many vicissitudes during this great span. Its surface has been moulded repeatedly by more recent agencies, some of them continuing today to produce an entrancing scenery. In places, this natural landscape remains unimpaired by recent events, but much of it has by now been artificially changed.

The several cultural waves which spread across Europe in the past have left successive imprints though here, on the remote fringe of the continent, their overlay is thin. The oppressive impact of the Industrial Revolution is much less than in the rest of Europe so that the many successive layers of antiquity remain visible to a greater extent than elsewhere, and much still remains of these various growth stages in the Irish landscape. Its features fall into a number of categories: the hard rock foundations; the surface and its morphology; the rich vegetation cover; the first human clearings many millennia ago.

4

Finally, the present man-made aspects of the landscape, and the peoples who settled it, are very much a part of the whole.

1. Foundations of the Landscape

Connemara, Mayo, the Ox Mountains, Donegal and Tyrone: these are the oldest parts of Ireland whose rocks initially accumulated as muds, sands and limestones in a primaeval sea and subsequently depressed deep into the earth's crust, became recrystallised (metamorphic) so that they are now glittering schists, sparkling quartzites and marbles. In such extreme circumstances rocks can flow in a plastic way quite different from their behaviour at the earth's surface and they are now often streaky, contorted gneisses as a result, whose surfaces, smoothed by the passage of ice sheets over them in much later times, crop out plentifully beneath the peat which is such a constant aspect of the west Ireland scene.

Quartzites are indurated rocks, intractable to weathering, and they produce the impressive pyramidal peaks and jagged knife-edge ridges which are so prominent in Errigal and Muckish, in the Twelve Pins and Nephin. Other quartzites which in the west form Croagh Patrick and in the east the Sugarloafs of Wicklow are of rather younger age. They appear among the Irish slate formations, themselves metamorphic though to a lesser degree than the schists and gneisses. Slate has a distinctive fissility (slaty cleavage), and slate country is characterised by pleasant rolling uplands. It occurs in a great belt reaching from Down to Cavan, again in east Leinster, in the cores of the smaller hill ranges of central and southern Ireland: Slieve Bloom, Slievenamon, the Knockmealdowns, the hills of Clare and others.

The igneous rock granite, too, is a product of the deep earth's crust; its intrusive domes and cauldrons formed some miles below surface in most cases, and they are now revealed by long denudation of their cover. It is a coarse-grained rock with the individual minerals readily distinguishable to the eye. In fact, the big veins of white pegmatite which traverse it sometimes carry enormous crystals: creamy felspars a foot or more long, big silvery 'books' of mica, and less common black tourmalines, green beryls and pink garnets.

The most wide-ranging structures in all these rocks are sets of joints, more or less regularly-arranged fractures which control their breakdown into boulders. Granite is a tough rock which forms some of Ireland's finest mountain land in the Wicklows, Blackstairs, Mournes and Bluestacks. In the warmer, moister climate of Tertiary times which preceded the recent Ice Age, it was very susceptible to chemical rotting and there are other granite areas – Galway, Ardara and the Rosses in Donegal, the Tullow region south of the Wicklows – where it has been reduced to subdued lowland as a result.

The most widespread and most familiar of Irish rock formations are the sedimentary Old Red Sandstone and the Carboniferous Limestone which, at four hundred million years and younger in age, have been spared the metamorphic events of the older rocks. In the south of Ireland these two great series, some miles thickness *in toto*, were involved in powerful earth movements, so that they are now disposed in the series of enormous fold arches and troughs which has produced the east-west morphological grain of Munster. Broad backs to the Old Red Sandstone folds develop our country's southern mountain ranges, warm-tinted though barren highlands, which include some of Ireland's highest and wildest peaks. The younger Carboniferous Limestone which overlay them has been removed by erosion, but it remains in the narrow troughs which lie in between, the rich lowland valleys of Munster.

The layered nature of these rocks (bedding or stratification) is clearly evident on the ground. Deep red tints to the sandstones, which give the formation its common name, mark the 'Old Red' as the accumulation of an ancient desert region. In contrast, the succeeding limestone formed on a warm, shallow sea floor, as is revealed by its multitudes of beautifully preserved fossil creatures: long-extinct sea-lilies, sea-mats, corals, lamp-shells and others. They crowd the bedding surfaces in the coastal cliffs of Hook Head and Bundoran, presenting a vivid and little-disturbed picture of that ancient sea-floor two hundred and fifty million years ago. Passing northwards from Munster the fold structures gradually die out and flat limestone underlies the monotonous Central Lowlands – ill-drained and hidden under a blanket of young glacial deposits and peats. In the west this formation rises in the high region of the Burren where the special features of limestone topography are strikingly developed.

Limestone, almost uniquely, is water-soluble to a significant degree. The amount of calcareous crust which deposits inside kettles in limestone districts is clear evidence of how much lime can be taken into solution. As the rain water soaks down along and enlarges joint cracks to leave grotesquely-etched limestone pavement above, the loose soil dries out and disappears, producing a rock desert where vegetation is confined to crevices and protected pockets.

Solution activity proceeds and enlarges joints to gaping grykes so that the subsurface formations are gradually honeycombed with great cavernous passages through which the water flows in underground rivers down to as far as percolation can reach. Here and there wholesale removal of the rock has produced extensive open depressions in the landscape, some of which hold permanent water-solution lakes such as Loughs Corrib and Mask, and Lough Leane in Killarney. In other cases these are most of the time dry, grassy flats ('turloughs', from *tuarloch*, 'a dried-up lake') which in wet weather suddenly become inundated as broad expanses of water are formed. Where they are not too far removed from the coastline some of these land-locked lakes have a tidal rise and fall as eloquent testimony to the cavernous nature of the limestone in which they lie.

Limestone country has a wonderful range of curious landscape features. Abandoned underground river channels are represented by caves with their spectacular growths of tufa, a limestone deposited from the hard waters in the form of drooping stalactites from the roofs and matching, upward-reaching stalagmite growths. The Mitchelstown caves in Tipperary and Dunmore caves in Kilkenny are notable examples. Some of them were hyaena dens in the remote past, into which these wild scavengers brought a variety of their food remains: deer, wolves, brown bears, with baby mammoths a conspicuous delicacy. Their larger parents were too big to be shifted, it seems, for they are absent from the masses of chewed bones buried in the cave floors.

Where parts of the cave roofs have fallen there are collapse gorges in which the rivers, once concealed, now flow in daylight. Swallow holes into which the surface streams suddenly disappear are numerous, as are resurgences where, conversely, underground rivers well out at the surface. Armed with the relevant Ordnance Survey Sheet one may enjoy a quiet walk in the vicinity of Yeats' famed Thoor Ballylee amid a whole succession of these features. The Devil's Punchbowl is a fine swallow hole in this district; another is the Shannon Pot in Co. Cavan from which Ireland's largest river first emerges into the open.

In the north of the country sandstone and shale horizons

are also present in the Carboniferous formations which rise high in the topography to produce the spectacular table mountains of Sligo and Leitrim: Ben Bulbin and the Bricklieve Mountains in the limestone, Cuilcagh and others in the sandstone. Here, and in the less striking Castlecomer and Slieveardagh plateaux in the south, coal seams and ironstone bands are present also (hence Slieve Anierin, 'the iron mountain') though not in quantities sufficient to support a heavy industry today. Paradoxically though, because of their unusual geological situation, Ireland's coal mines, such as they are, operate not from the earth's deep recesses but from high up in the hills. Where similar structural conditions occur at the coastline they give rise to striking cliff scenery. South Clare has, in the Cliffs of Moher, the greatest range of sheer rock faces in western Europe; Fair Head in Co. Antrim is similarly impressive.

North-east Ireland (Co. Antrim and the Lagan and Bann Valleys) is a quite distinctive part of the country. Protected under a great pile of basalt lava flows, and largely hidden by them, is a series of younger sedimentary formations: Chalk, Lias Clays, and the desert-formed New Red Sandstone, which are familiar elements in south England's landscape but are restricted to the north-east of this country. Antrim's Chalk cliffs are a replica of those which guard St George's Channel. The flint nodules within the white limestone, present solely in this part of Ireland, were the raw materials for the flint knappers in the early years of the human era, and the products of their factories along the coast at Larne, Whitepark Bay and elsewhere travelled widely over Ireland.

But everywhere in this region the dominant surface rock is dark, oily-coloured basalt lava: in buildings, in quarries, in coastal cliffs. Its succession of flows, individually a score or so of feet thick, build up to a pile totalling thousands of feet, and about sixty million years ago this represented a style of volcanism akin to that which is active in Hawaii today. Gases frothed from the hot lava surfaces to give vesicles which soon filled with lovely crystals of zeolites as well as chalcedony and opal. When the cooling was regular individual flows often shrank into a honeycomb pattern of cracks perpendicular to their surfaces. These peculiar structures have made the Giant's Causeway an object of world fame.

Basalt lavas form the surfaces of the high plateau but at its south-west extremity crustal rifting has dropped them down in a deep fault trough, its floor more than a thousand feet below sea level, to form the site of Ireland's biggest lake, Lough Neagh. It has filled up with sediment long since, so that the 153 square mile expanse is now shallow water and shows little evidence of its structural origin. On the other side of the plateau conditions along the coastal cliffs make for large-scale instability at many places and it is a typical landslide area. The soft clays of the Lias formation often occur at the base of the cliffs and surface water percolating down into these causes them to slide and flow under the big load of Chalk and basalt on top. As a result dislocated blocks of the plateau, some of them many acres in area, have in the past slipped down seawards. The Larne promontory is a major example and at Garron Tower others are very prominent, while on a lesser scale the cascading slips of clay even today pose a threat to the Antrim coast road in wet weather so that it requires constant surveillance.

2. Surface and Morphology

The hard rock formations constitute the country's foundations and they control, broadly, the character of its surface. But the topography of the land has been shaped by quite different factors than those which formed its rocks and, though ancient in human terms, these are a great deal younger. They are the processes of weathering and erosion. Rivers are responsible for the latter as they deepen their channels and extend the ramifications of the drainage system until it involves the whole landscape. Just as the run-off from a rain shower carves little gullies in any exposed soil surface, in the long term the landscape is removed piecemeal until the ultimate result is a featureless, low-lying peneplain. An original high land surface will, in time, disappear in this way except for a few of its upland remnants, and at length the only trace of it which remains may be found in scattered hill summits which accord with one another in level. They were, after all, once part of a continuous landscape.

This sequence of events is slow indeed to run to completion and a new uplift of the land may intervene to re-elevate the topography so that the whole erosion cycle is started anew. There may in fact be repeated uplifts and, as a consequence, many landscapes register several of these distinct levels in their topography. Calary plateau is a familiar example of an uplifted erosion surface and, above it, the rolling uplands which top much of the Wicklows, the Featherbed, for example, are the fragmentary remains of older, higher levels. Great flat expanses at 100-200 feet O.D. covered with blanket bog dominate much of western Ireland, and in Ulster the rolling uplands of south Armagh at an even level around 400 feet are equally emphatic surfaces. Compared with its earlier geological history these are much more recent phases in the country's evolution, and since the processes still operate it is their effects which dominate Ireland's landscapes today. As regards the rate at which they work we must think in terms of millions of years instead of the hundreds of millions represented by the more ancient rock formations.

For the latest elements in Ireland's landscape the time perspective shortens still further. These are the scenic details which have originated in the last 100,000 years or so, in the nature of a retouch to the overall landform. The lowlands are dominated by the effects of great ice sheets, thousands of feet thick perhaps, during most of this time while in the mountains there were more restricted valley glaciers fed from higher-level ice-caps. The former left an undulating cover of their ground moraine, namely boulder clay, thick over central Ireland and fertile from its content of limestone pebbles, if not generally free-draining.

Sometimes, where there was a lot of it, patches of this ill-sorted material stagnated beneath the moving ice and were moulded into oval mounds by the sheet passing over them. These are the drumlins which form a great belt across the north Midlands from Donegal to Downpatrick. There are no easy passages for outgoing drainage through this jumbled mass of small hills, the so-called 'basket of eggs' topography, and many swampy lakes fill the depressions between them, producing the typical landscape of counties Cavan and Monaghan, the Irish Lakelands.

In the declining stages of the glacial epoch great quantities of melt water flooded the low ground. Wherever this was held up gravels, sands and muds, washed out of the boulder clay, settled in temporary lakes the abandoned sites of which are seen today as flat-bottomed old lake basins. Such is 'Glacial Lake Blessington', the area which now holds the modern reservoir, and the gravel-filled basin of the old 'Glacial Lake Enniskerry' on the opposite side of the northern end of the Wicklow mountains. These floods, too, spread a gravel and sand wash out from the receding ice-front which, at the local points of discharge, often developed into long, ribbon-like ridges running for miles across country: the eskers strikingly seen around Tullamore and in many other parts of central Ireland.

Glacial activity, however, was generally in the nature

of erosion of the surfaces over which the ice sheets passed. Even the very toughest materials such as the granite crags at Killiney Hill on the outskirts of Dublin, or the red sandstones of west Cork and Kerry, have been smoothed off, scratched and deeply scored by the great mass of overriding ice as their outcrop forms today so well reflect. Geographers apply the quaint French term *roche moutonné*, literally 'sheep rocks' to such round-backed outlines.

Mountain valleys such as Glendalough and others in the east Wicklows; Anascaul, Caragh and many in Kerry; as well as those of the hill regions of Mayo, Donegal and the Mournes, have a characteristic U-shaped profile where they were greatly enlarged by the passage of massive ice streams along their channels. As a result, side tributaries now spill into them over the high lip which exists at each side, in picturesque waterfalls, and here and there basins in their broad floors hold pretty lakes: Caragh Lake, Glendalough, Lough Dan and many others. Crescentic moraines of boulder clay are festooned conspicuously across the valley bottoms wherever a glacier snout halted temporarily, and where finally melt water was ponded back in these valley areas its overflow often found ways to escape sideways by cutting deep rocky spillways through a lateral ridge. The latter remains are the peculiar Dry Gaps so common in hill areas. The wild, mile-long Pass of Keimaneigh through the Sheehy Mountains in West Cork is the most impressive, while many will know the deep defile of the Glen-of-the-Downs traversed by the main road south from Dublin.

Mountain areas had their individual ice caps from which valley glaciers were fed and where, after the lowland ice had gone, local snow patches, backed against the higher slopes, remained long enough to rot their way down into sunken pockets whose forms remain as bowl-shaped amphitheatres or coombes, sometimes very large and deep, remote, and often filled with lonely corrie lakes. Greatest of the latter is the spectacular Coomshingaun in the Waterford Comeraghs. Mangerton Lake in Kerry and the twin Loughs Bray in Wicklow are also well-known.

The last 10,000 years (post-Glacial times) saw the formation of the youngest features in the landscape, scenic details for the most part rather than major aspects, freshly delineated and often impressive because of this. During this time the flora and fauna were restored to the land, and as the climate gradually evolved towards that of today the vegetation cover, too, became progressively modified.

For most of it conditions were suitable for human occupation and man appeared here perhaps 9000 years ago. For the latter half of the period his impact has been sufficient to modify the environment very much indeed.

The youngest features of Ireland's rivers will be found in their upper reaches, through which the channel has only recently extended and where the torrents flow in a deep, narrow valley via a succession of cataracts. Their lower courses are older, smoother, and with gentler gradients. Here the valley floor has opened out over a flat spread of gravel and sand – a flood plain across which the channel courses to and fro in a series of meanders. A recent uplift would, of course, increase the stream gradient and hence eroding power, and a similar effect might result from a change in volume of the flow. In such cases channels in the flood plain are deepened to leave conspicuous terraces high on each side. This may lead to rivers incising their courses so as to form series of rock-cut gorges as, for instance, in the picturesque middle reaches of the Barrow and the Nore, the Boyne Valley lower down its course, the Dargle Glen and many others.

As must be expected in an island outpost, Ireland's coastal scenery is impressive and varied: cliffs in a range of forms, great sandy beaches with extensive lagoons to their rear, drowned inlets and swollen tidal estuaries, as well as deep-going fjord-like indentations. On steep coasts the keynote of activity is erosion, and cliff scenery is the outcome. Waves break close inshore and their rollers beat constantly on the cliff bases so that these retreat steadily inland.

In contrast, where coasts are shallow the breakers develop far out and expend their energy piling up sand in offshore sand-bars. Winds blow the surfaces of these into high dunes and tidal creeks are cut off behind, the haunt of multitudes of wildfowl. With progressive reclamation these wetlands, in some cases the last remaining hope of survival for migratory bird species such as the Greenland goose in the Wexford Slobs, are fast disappearing. Many of the low coastlines are great sandy beaches stretching away out of sight in the distance for as much as ten miles in south Wexford (Ballyteigue) and Derry (Magilligan).

In Ice Age times the amount of water taken up in the continental ice sheets was such that sea levels the world over were lower by hundreds of feet than they are today. Europe's Atlantic coastline then reached unbroken from Portugal to points off the west coast of Ireland and Ireland, with England, was part of the continental mainland. When the ice melted seas were everywhere flooded, the continental shelf islands became isolated as levels rose, and gradually the waters spread up the large river mouths in extensive tidal estuaries. This produced in the swollen lower reaches of south-east Ireland's major rivers such as the Suir, Nore, Barrow and Slaney, a characteristic aspect.

The island's boundary is a drowned coastline of this sort and in regions of varied topography the effects on its scenery are both diverse and spectacular. The hilly coasts around Cork city enclose a whole complex of deep and far-reaching inlets. More striking and, indeed, classical from the geographer's point of view, is the region further west of this where the mountain lands of southern Ireland head straight out to sea at the extremities of Cork and Kerry. Here the highland ridges are a succession of rugged salients which tail off in rocky islets after ranging thirty miles and more into the Atlantic: Bantry, Kenmare, Dingle and the others. Between them are broad, deep-going inlets ending in fertile sheltered farmland where the low limestone basins channel the main rivers seawards.

In the crystalline terrain of the north and west of the country jagged quartzite ranges meet the Atlantic in some of the wildest cliff scenery to be found anywhere: Croaghaun (Achill) and Slieve League (Donegal) both have faces dropping two thousand feet straight into the ocean. In a less emphatic manner this scenic pattern is repeated elsewhere on Ireland's coastline. The low, rocky headlands of north Dublin, for example, alternate with broader, sand-barred inlets at Baldoyle, Malahide and Portraine. Deep inlets of a different sort, more akin to the spectacular Norwegian fjords, are the few examples further north where highlands with former glaciated valleys reach the sea, namely the fjord-like glaciated valleys of Carlingford on the east and Killary on the west.

The ten millennia, or about four hundred generations, which have elapsed since ice sheets finally left Ireland must seem an enormous span in terms of human life, but it is a trifle compared with the aeons of time involved in our country's evolution. None-the-less, the interplay of climatic change, vegetation and landscape development, and human activities which took place during this short period make it the most significant and most interesting part of Ireland's story. When rising sea levels finally broke the continental links around 8000 years ago Ireland and England achieved their modern outlines. Their flora and fauna, however, evolved somewhat differently. Ireland has some surprising plants and animals: southern or

Mediterranean forms, which are relics of the time when the Irish coastline was one with that of the Iberian peninsula. The strawberry tree (*Arbutus*) so distinctive in the Killarney woods, is otherwise found no nearer than Spain and this is the case too with the spotted slug (*Geomalacus*). Our location as an island more remote than Britain from mainland Europe has made its recolonisation even less complete than that of our sister island which, in turn, is notably poorer than that of Europe. Several familiar creatures such as moles and dormice failed to reach this land, as did all of the snakes for, whatever tradition may say about the role of our patron saint, they were in fact too slow moving to complete the voyage ahead of the rising sea.

Most widespread of these recent events has been the growth of peats. Peat studies, and those of the foetid muds at lake bottoms, are crucial in elucidating the evolution of post-Glacial vegetation and, with it, climatic change. These deposits preserve the pollen which is discharged in great amounts by flowering plants and, since different pollens are readily identified, the peat succession in a bog holds evidence of the vegetation and climatic changes as it accumulated. They show that conditions have varied much since the ice left Ireland. At first it was an unattractive place: a cold barren tundra with mosses and arctic shrubs such as we see today in the Scandinavian highlands. It could, however, support the giant Irish deer (*Megaloceras*) in considerable numbers, for at the base of many bogs are muds with the remains of arctic plants and it is these that often contain the 'Irish Elk' skeletons. A few species with arctic affinities such as the Irish Hare are with us still. But climate improved steadily and after a thousand years was capable of supporting the first modern forests of pine and spruce, a taiga such as we see in Finland today. The remains of these oldest forests are to be seen here and there in our bogs as a multitude of pine stumps (bog deal) still rooted *in situ* in the sands at the base of the peat.

The climate was rather better in those days than it is now and these remains often appear where no trees grow today, such as high up on the Featherbed Mountain in Wicklow or out on the bleak windswept lands of Mayo. In fact, Ireland's modern conifers are recent reintroductions since the native Irish pine had disappeared already in prehistoric times. As climate steadily improved the conifers were replaced by deciduous hardwoods: mixed oak, ash, elm forests; they would be the natural vegetation of

14

the Irish lowlands today. About 6000 years ago the climate reached its optimum, considerably warmer and moister than it is now, and it has oscillated quite a bit since then. The bulk of peat growth took place during the moister phases of the past, between 4000-6000 years ago, and again around the turn of the Christian era. Ireland's climate is now somewhat drier and colder; little peat grows and, in fact, on exposed hillsides it is often seen to be eroding.

Ireland's bogs are either raised 'red' bog or blanket bog. Raised bog occurs extensively in the waterlogged terrain of the Central Lowlands with its impeded drainage. There the bog mosses act as a gigantic sponge and so build up in the centre to a level well above that of the surrounding countryside. Blanket bog develops as a continuous layer of peat wherever rainfall exceeds about fifty inches annually and so it ranges down to sea level on the west coast, rising higher on the mountains in the east of the country. The great barren wastes of north Mayo typify blanket bog, while a view from Croghan Hill, almost dead centre, geographically, in Ireland yields an impressive vista of raised bog, in this case the great Bog of Allen.

3. The Green Mantle

For a visitor the most memorable aspect of the Irish landscape is likely to be the luxuriance and variety of its plant life. Unfortunately, little or nothing remains of the original land cover in more fertile areas. The drift-covered plains and moderately-elevated uplands have been under agriculture for centuries and only in the poorer ground can one see something of the character of its natural vegetation. Another striking feature is the way in which tree growth is almost entirely inhibited over a broad belt along the Atlantic seaboard. Along the roadsides blasted hawthorn trees seem to lean uniformly inland since the salt winds have trimmed their western sides. Some sheltered sites, such as Connemara's lake islets, hidden in depressions, and the wizened stands of oakwood behind Croagh Patrick and Old Head, hold the few remnants of native wood in this great expanse of bare ground. Yet in the better climatic conditions of the past these parts were densely covered by coniferous forest, and cutaway bogs often expose great numbers of *in situ* stumps, which grew anything up to 7000 years ago, rooted in the soil beneath.

The oakwoods of Killarney around Lough Leane, those in Donegal by Lough Easke, and the woods west of Lough

15 *continued on page 32* ▶

The Dublin Coastline

For many visitors the first view of Ireland, as their plane wings towards Dublin airport, is the subdued coastline of north Dublin. The Central Lowlands here extend seawards in the familiar pattern of a drowned coastline (see p. 17) but, in contrast to the rugged outlines of the west, this is a gentler topography with altogether milder shores. The river divides are low headlands, cut back at their noses in rocky cliffs. From each of them, sand-bars extend to block the intervening estuaries, now filled by tidal mud-flats and developing salt-marshes. In the receding distance are, respectively, Baldoyle estuary, the Velvet strand, Portmarnock promontory, Malahide estuary, Portraine point, Rogerstown estuary, Rush. Unspectacular landscape, all of it, yet enormously interesting to the naturalist with its range of vegetation types in dunes and salt-marsh, its wealth of aquatic birds, its profusion of fossils in the limestone formations and its interesting volcanic structures in the lavas further afield.

Ancient rocks: quartzites and slates, volcanics, granites, in turn form the craggy island massifs of Howth and Ireland's Eye, Lambay, Rockabill. The first of these is now linked to the Dublin mainland by a sandy isthmus at Sutton and it has been so since the first Mesolithic settlers in the district left the remains of their encampment there 5,250 years ago. The coastline has risen since, and the Raheny road lies on beach deposits about twelve feet above high water level with the old shore further inland. The broad sweep of Dublin Bay has Bull Island as its most recent feature. The Bull Wall delimiting it on the south was erected in 1819 to restrict the Liffey discharge so that its scour would maintain the navigable channel. Sand has accumulated in the calmer water to the north only since then, forming the four-mile-long sand spit with dune belt, salt-marsh, and tidal lagoon behind, famous internationally as a wild bird santuary.

A Wicklow Valley

Glendalough is one of Ireland's most famous beauty spots, deep
ened to a broad, steep-walled profile by a glacier which de
scended from the distant granite highlands. Out of sight at the
valley head a sharp declivity marks the point where the ice stream
commenced: its gathering ground was the snow fields in the
higher mountains above. Today the scenic contrast between
these mature rolling uplands and the valley sharply cut into them
is impressive. As it wound down-valley the glacier truncated a
lateral spur of mica-schists projecting from our left in the middle
distance. In the rock face which resulted, the little crevice known
as St Kevin's Bed is reputed to have served as a penitential
retreat, more than 1,400 years ago, for Ireland's best-loved saint.
The glacial overdeepening is also reflected in a high tributary
stream from the south, the Pollanass brook, which drops into the
main valley in a picturesque cataract, hence in Gaelic *Poll-an-eas*
'the hole of the waterfall'.

In the valley floor at this point a broad gravel fan has built up

where the little brook debouches, and it now separates the Upper and Lower lakes (Gleann-da-loch, 'the Glen of the Two Lakes'). In the foreground another raised gravel fan, produced by the Glendasan stream, whose hidden entry is from the right-hand side, provided the site of the main twelfth-thirteenth-century walled monastic town, whose round tower is prominent among the pines which hide its other remains. But the earlier monastic site was up-valley on the Pollanass gravel spread, where lie the scattered remains of many early crosses and bullauns, a cashel, a lochán, and the tenth-century Reefert church set in the ancient burial ground of the medieval chieftains of eastern Wicklow.

The first settlement of all was eremetical in character, remote and lonely, on the inaccessible valley slopes beyond the upper lake. Oak-woods, remnants of the ancient deciduous woodland which was the natural vegetation of much of the sheltered lowlands, clothe the southern slopes; conifer plantations occupy the other side.

Fair Head

Antrim's coast provides the most varied of geological panorama
in Ireland. There are white Chalk cliffs near Portrush where the
sea has carved from them the Wishing Arch. Basalt lavas cover
most of the plateau inland and appear coastally with their exqui-
site honeycomb jointing, which has made the Giant's Causeway
scenically famous. Beneath these formations is the soft, grey Lias
Clay which, turgid with ground water, has heaved and flowed in a
variety of spectacular landslides from Larne northwards, capsizing
great blocks of the massive rocks above.

The county's north-eastern corner is different once again.
There the flat Carboniferous formations are warm yellow
sandstones, interbedded with black seams of coal high up on the
nearer slopes, where adits have been driven horizontally into the
cliffs to work them. This view looks north-eastwards from near
Ballycastle across to Fair Head, where a thick sheet, or sill, of the
dark basaltic magma injected itself along the Carboniferous
strata. Its vertical joints now outline the cliff faces and a great
scree of fallen-away dolerite boulders slopes down from the foot
of it.

The high ground above is flat moorland with a crannog
studded lake or two. Desolate now, it none-the-less supported
flourishing agricultural communities in Neolithic and later times,
their farming and settlement patterns abundantly preserved under the peat. The cliff coast is the haunt of sea birds and, in
particular, raptors, for there the golden eagle has nested in recent
years and buzzards are regularly to be seen.

A Cashel View

Geological and historical aspects, each in their own way, gove[rn]
the landscape of south Tipperary. Great fold arches of the eas[t]
west Armorican mountains – nearly 300 million years old – for[m]
the backbones of the Galtees, Slievenaman and others of th[e]
Munster ranges; they abut the Central Ireland lowlands of fl[at]
Carboniferous Limestone. The wild and barren hill ranges [to]
south, rich agricultural lowlands, deeply spread with glac[ial]
deposits, to the north. Supported on a conspicuous box-shape[d]
fold in the bedded limestones – an outlier of the major mounta[in]
structures – the Rock of Cashel raises its majestic ruins clear [of]
modern Cashel's tasteless scatter of buildings below and domi[n]
ates the plain.

Cashel, 'The Stone Fort', was already a royal site of Munst[er]
when Patrick visited it in the fifth century. Traditionally, this [is]
where, seeking to illustrate the mystery of the Trinity, the sai[nt]
plucked the shamrock leaf which has become our national e[m]
blem. We are told, too, how during the baptism his crosi[er]
accidentally transfixed the king's foot, a trial which the latter bo[re]

unflinchingly as he imagined it to be part of the ritual. This became the major centre of the South — both secular and ecclesiastical — and many of its bishops coming from the ruling family of Munster ruled as kings. The opulence of its remains reflects this, and it is in marked contrast to the lonely austerity of our older monastic sites.

The boundary wall of the modern graveyard outlines the ancient stronghold, which became church property in 1101. Its early ruins — the cross, the round tower and the lovely little Hiberno-Romanesque church — date from this century. The more expansive cathedral, archbishop's castle and residence of the attendant clergy (Hall of the Vicars' Choral) are thirteenth century and later. Our view westwards from the precincts atop the Rock is across the rich, grassy farmland with the thirteenth-century Cistercian Hore Abbey nearby; far away, the Galtees, almost blotted out by a summer rainstorm, rise abruptly from the plain.

The Burren

In the Burren hills, rising to just over 1,000 feet, Co. Clare has the finest development of bare limestone plateau in all of northern Europe. The Carboniferous Limestone here is a pure, grey rock, thick-bedded and flat, abounding in corals, molluscs and other fossils that lived in the warm, shallow seas where it accumulated over 300 million years ago. Steeper scarp slopes face to the north, but the general stratification of this formation can be seen in well-defined lines which tilt gently southwards. As a result, overlying shales and flags appear at the surface in this direction, around Lisdoonvarna and over south-west Clare, where they meet the sea in Moher's towering cliffs.

The limestone plateau is barren rock desert today, etched by solution into fantastic shapes and gaping fissures (grykes) along enlarged joints; but in sheltered nooks and crevices a little soil permits the development of its rich and distinctive flora. Surface

water drains quickly into it and so the landscape is bone dry, but this water reappears lower down to irrigate the terrain in the foregound, where clayey glacial drift supports rich grassland and patches of deciduous wood. This is the typical stone wall country where the Central Lowlands reach west to Galway Bay, a region almost overwhelmed by the rich cream colours of May-blossom along the hedgerows in early summer.

Here, from Ballyvaughan round by Kinvarra and Gort, is low ground with a profusion of the peculiar features of limestone country, where streams disappear abruptly into swallets to emerge at resurgences some way on; where little gorge-like valleys, blind at each end, mark the falling-in of limestone caverns; and shallow grassy depressions (turloughs) may suddenly become extensive lakes after a night of rain.

The Cliffs of Moher

The bare rock Carboniferous Limestone plateau of north Clare gives way southwards to poor, wet uplands, where flat beds of sandstone and shale follow on top of the limestone and form a high tableland. The sandstones, Liscannor Flags, accumulated as the deposits of a sandy coastline about 300 million years ago. They are now a popular decorative stone because of the many tortuous worm casts which diversify the bedding surfaces, the counterparts of what one sees on beaches today at low tide.

This range of sheer coastal cliffs, unbroken for more than eight miles, is amongst Europe's most impressive. They clearly show how the deep water allows Atlantic waves to break virtually at the cliff base where they cut into the soft black shales with

ease, so that vertical, joint-bounded masses of the more durable sandstones become undermined and fall away. The waves sweep in in a series of bow-shaped fronts, and hence the cliffs which they develop present a succession of cusps and embayments to the ocean. The little sea stack is a remnant which has survived from a time when their line lay further west than its limits today.

On top of the cliffs is the early nineteenth-century tower built as a tea house by the landlord of this district, Cornelius O'Brien MP, at the point where the cliffs reach a maximum elevation of 668 feet.

Connemara

Two factors in particular produce the distinctive Connemara landscape with its rugged mountains and wide stretches of flat bog. It is forged from a variety of ancient crystalline rocks, the Dalradian formations: granites, schists, locally decorative types such as the rare Connemara Marble, and quartzites, which recur in Donegal and again in Highland Scotland, giving a unity of character to these widely separated regions. In particular, tough quartzites produce upstanding, rugged mountains with characteristic pyramidal peaks, while less resistant rocks form the lower ground.

Quartzite highlands form the background of this Clifden panorama, but a second aspect of it, the presence of several conspicuous levels in its topography, is still more impressive. The distant quartzite mountains, some of them flat-topped, accord to

an even level above 2,000 feet O.D. It was produced in the remote past by the wearing down of the landscape to a low-lying, flat peneplain, subsequently uplifted to present altitude. Other younger, and lower, erosion surfaces can be made out in the middle distance and in the foreground. The little tidal creek which reaches up to Clifden village is a part of our country's system of drowned coastlines produced about 8,000 years ago when, as the ice sheets melted, the sea level rose and flooded the valley mouths.

Clifden shelters in the lower ground where, in marked contrast to the exposed terrain all around, deciduous trees flourish reasonably well. It was the creation of a local landlord early last century and, for a time, was a railway terminus.

The Barrow below Graiguenamanagh

This is a distinctive Co. Carlow panorama made up of a variety of landscape elements. The distant granite hills of Mount Leinster (furthest away) and the nearer Blackstairs are typically rounded with a few granite tors atop them, exposed nunataks which protruded above the former ice-sheets and so weathered sub-aerially. The single ridge lies at the eastern margin of the big Leinster granite body, the main part of which, in the middle distance, has been worn down to a smooth, drift-covered platform. This occurred in the warm, wet climate of Tertiary times before the onset of the Ice Age, for the tough igneous rock decomposes readily in these circumstances and was easily removed so that the landscape developed into a low, even peneplain.

This is a part of Ireland's geological history on which we are little informed, for our country was already land when the younger sedimentary rocks were being laid down in shallow seas over the present English lowlands, but where this surface extends into central Ireland there are a few hidden patches of Tertiary sediment resting on it to define its age. It was uplifted later as a

conspicuous level platform in the landscape of Carlow. The Irish term *greach,* 'a flat upland place', in the place-name 'Graigue-namanagh' may emphasise this distinctive aspect of the scenery.

The same plateau reaches the sea in the cliff coastline of Waterford, and into it the three main rivers in south-east Ireland's drainage system have sharply incised their courses as picturesque gorges. A final chapter in the evolution of this scene was written when the flooding seas of end-Ice Age times spread far up their valleys. The Barrow is tidal to St Mullins as a consequence, just a few miles below this point, and even within our view the valley floor is a narrow flood-plain of deposited silt. A canal with towpath supplements a difficult stretch of river whose depth is maintained by a weir. The damp water-meadows are rush-grown, while craggy slopes of the gorge are largely under gorse or furze. Above it, the large fields suggest prosperous farms, and hedgerows armed with briars complete the scene.

Conn in Mayo are examples of the deciduous forest which represents the natural vegetation of Ireland's lowlands. The sheltered valleys of east Wicklow: Clara, Glendalough and Glen of the Downs, are others. Such woods have the characteristic ground flora which marks centuries-old, primary forests. Plants such as bluebell, wood sorrel and wood anemone are suited to this habitat because they flower before the leaf canopy has developed and so produce a wealth of colour in springtime. Around them, too, are still scattered some of the economically-unattractive tree species, such as holly and crab apple which remain as outliers of woodland in former times. Many place-names, such as Derry, Ros (as in Rosnaree), and others, reflect the once-extensive spread of this great forest, and one notes that these relate to the better-drained parts of the lowlands (marsh and bog inhibited its growth), and to sheltered valleys, for the exposed uplands seem to have been devoid of trees.

But the famous woods of Medieval times: the Dufrey in Wexford and the Royal Forest of Glencree near Dublin, have long gone, and everything that remains has been modified a great deal by human interference. Artificial grassland now dominates this natural setting and such common trees as ash, hawthorn, blackthorn and cherry are seldom found except where planted in hedgerows, where they mingle with such imports as horse chestnut, beech and poplar. In secondary woodland the more vigorous nettles, brambles and bracken tend to oust more colourful primary herbs. Some distinctive facets of the forest assemblage remain very localised, such as the hazel thickets on drained limey areas of the lowlands, e.g. the esker ridges near Tullamore and Tyrellspass in the midlands, and the groves of birch and rowan in upland hollows, but there must be others which we can no longer adequately recreate.

Wherever Carboniferous Limestone rises sufficiently high in the topography to be free-draining and clear of glacial deposits, it forms a spectacular, naked-rock landscape with a quite unusual flora. The limestone plateau of the Burren in north Clare, roughly 120 square miles in area, is the most important cool-temperate limestone region in Europe, and there are smaller, less emphatic occurrences in the table mountains of Sligo, Leitrim and Roscommon as well as around Lough Gur in Limerick. The density of prehistoric settlement in such areas is often impressive and certainly the elaborate ancient field systems attached to many of the Clare cashels would be quite out of place in today's barren environment. In fact, it seems that in Iron Age times and earlier, the Burren was sufficiently clothed in soil to support vigorous agriculture.

Today, virtually without cover, it carries a rich and varied assemblage of plants, tucked away in clefts in its rocky platforms and in small grassy patches, whose blossoms produce a wonderful display throughout the warmer parts of the year. Distinctive lime-loving plants such as the blue spring gentian, bloody cranesbill and mossy saxifrage are associated in places with a range of orchids. Mountain avens, of arctic-alpine provenance, mingle with southern European forms such as the delicate maidenhair fern, and the natural hazel thickets here are the Irish stronghold of the rare pine-marten.

The low marshy country which flanks many of our major rivers inland is subject to seasonal flooding and is characterised by lush water meadows (or callows). Farming is precarious and hay-making is late, thus allowing many flowering plants and bird species to successfully complete the annual cycle of reproduction. They continue to flourish here, although gone from other former habitats. The Shannon, rated to be the longest river in Europe which remains unpolluted, has much outstanding callows environment in its middle reaches below Athlone. It is a rich grassland with a wealth of colourful flowers: the common buttercup, dandelion, ox-eye, sorrel, and the more distinctive meadowsweet and marsh cinquefoil. Its 'old' character is indicated by the presence of such plants as cowslip which has become rare in modern farmland. Bird migrants, the once-common corncrake, for example, manage to hold their own for the same reason. The assemblage is kept viable by the late mowing which local conditions necessitate and it is clear that with even a slight change in agricultural practice this attractive environment and its special survivors would be lost for ever.

Dune belts and salt-marsh are special coastal environments in which grasses or related plants play a major role in stabilising the new sedimentary accumulations. They are, in fact, part of the syndrome connected with drowned coastlines. The dune belts of Dundrum Bay in Co. Down and Bull Island in Dublin Bay will be familiar to many. At the seaward side of the dunes creeping grasses, whose stolons or rhizomes can spread along the loose sand and form a stable environment for plants, are typical. Nearest to the tide mark salt-tolerant sea couchgrass is usually the first prominent coloniser. Higher up, and out of reach of the sea water, marram grass takes over and the dunes may reach 150 feet in height. Behind this outer belt the sheltered leeway has varied grassland with mosses and a variety of flowering plants, maybe with clumps of alder, the home of larks and other small birds.

In brackish estuaries and muddy lagoons on the landward side of sandbars salt-marsh develops to reclaim the evolving mud-flats which are the haunt of great flocks of wading birds: dunlins, oyster-catchers, curlews, to mention a few, as well as a multitude of migratory ducks and geese. Again, the North Bull is an outstanding example, a nature reserve of international renown which exists literally within the limits of the capital city, and salt-marsh is also present in the other tidal inlets along the north Dublin coast. It is populated by halophytic, or salt-tolerant, plants and is covered for the major part at high tide. The succulent glasswort is the first coloniser on the mud flats to give a meadow type of vegetation but cordgrass, introduced to the Dublin marshes for reclamation purposes, now grows in conspicuous clumps as does sea lavender and sea plantain. Beyond high water limits rushes, sedges and grasses such as red fescue have taken over from the halophytes. Here too, but more typically on coastal cliffs, colonies of sea pinks locally give a profusion of colour in summer.

Machair (*machaire* in Irish means 'low flat country') is a Scots Gaelic word from the Western Isles which refers to a special type of plant environment occurring on exposed Atlantic coasts both there and along the west coast of Ireland. It arises on the old beach deposits which may extend considerable distances inland and carry a great deal of calcareous material: comminuted shells, pinhead skeletons of foraminifera, and coralline algae, the latter giving the misnomer 'coral strand' to some Connemara beaches. This is a grassland community of red fescue, smooth meadow grass, sweet vernal grass, cocksfoot, Yorkshire fog, false oat with clovers and a colourful range of wild flowers: yellow flags in damp places, silverweed, harebell, speedwell and many others. The machaire is common land and so has not been modified by improvement procedures, and hay-making is late enough to allow its bird population of corncrakes and larks, with waders such as lapwing, plover and oyster-catcher, to raise their broods successfully. Any change in conditions, however, is likely to eradicate this precarious environment.

Bogs, which are by far the most widespread type of natural vegetation remaining in Ireland, until recently occupied about one-sixth of the country. When the bogs began to form around 9000 years ago the many shallow lake basins present in the lowlands served as centres in which fen peat, made up of reeds, sedges and various water plants, started to form. As the lakes contracted and peat thickened, vegetation growing on the latter was blanketed off from the subsoil beneath and so became deprived of mineral constituents. Sphagnum moss, which can thrive virtually without inorganic materials, took over as a consequence and has produced the increasingly acid conditions which typify our modern bogs. The moss tussocks develop a hummocky surface interspersed with bog pools and support a very distinctive range of vegetation. Carniverous plants such as sundew and butterwort, get their nitrogen supplies from captured insects, while the shrubby tree growth, represented by clumps of bog myrtle, does so by producing root nodules in the manner of legumes. Dried-out surfaces are spread with heathers, the widespread ling and more restricted bell heather giving the delicate cover of purple and pink respectively to the boglands in August.

On mountains such as the Wicklows one can see a range of plant associations which typify various parts of these boglands. A moss tundra with great spread mounds of Rhacomitrium is found on exposed summits where erosion is active. Wet bogland, in contrast to the drier heather moors, supports a vegetation of low, spiky deer grass, golden brown in autumn, associated with waving spreads of white-tasselled bog cotton. Marshy seepages on hill slopes are mostly dominated by rushes, while drier scree is often colonised by fraochans (bilberries). At a lower level rocky ground and thin soils are a blaze of golden furze: the common gorse up to about 1000 feet before June, and the smaller or western gorse higher up in the hill pastures after July. Bracken fern is a rapid coloniser of neglected hill grassland today. In the lowlands, the Pollardstown fen in county Kildare, a feeder of the Grand Canal, is an example of fen-type bogland, the southern borders of Lough Neagh another.

Few parts of the land today remain in their original state. The high mountain moors, lowland bogs and marshes, coastal dunes and backwaters, are as we have seen largely unmodified by human activity. Among these one can recognise many places which were extensively worked by prehistoric farming peoples in better climates of the past but which, long since abandoned as unprofitable, have fully reverted to a natural state, for Ireland's evolution is clearly a dynamic process, continuing still.

The wild areas, however, are now almost everywhere under pressure from encroaching modern development: peat working, reclamation and land drainage, coastal exploitation for holiday use. It is a matter of the greatest concern to preserve even small pieces of these natural environments for the enlightenment of future generations.

4. Early Human Impact

It was some time after the ice disappeared that Ireland's continental links were severed, and climate and vegetation had developed to a level at which human settlement was possible. Mesolithic communities of food-gathering people travelled, perhaps across the narrow North Channel which separates the Rhinns of Galloway from Antrim, to become our first inhabitants some 9000 years ago. They spread in coastal settlements and by lakesides in the interior to colonise the country, living by hunting wild game, fishing and gathering wild plant food. The Neolithic settlers who arrived about four millennia later were our first farmers, and with their surprisingly efficient polished stone axes they were able to clear large areas of forest, to harvest crops, and to breed domestic stock. For the first time the human impact on the landscape was appreciable, and one can at this stage detect in the pollen record preserved in the peats a sharp reduction in the number of trees, which is clearly as a result of tree felling. This is coupled with an important increase in grasses and weeds which are typical of open ground: plantain, dock and others.

Indeed, more equable climates enabled the succeeding Bronze Age communities, about 2000 BC, to construct their fields and to farm extensively in many places where it is no longer profitable, for these remains are found beneath the endless bogs of Mayo, and at levels in the Blackstairs and Wicklows many hundreds of feet above where farms and habitations extend today. The bare limestone pavements of the Burren were then populous terrain: old field boundaries stretch across them for miles, and stone-walled cashel habitations and megalithic burial sites are everywhere to be seen.

The settlements of our Mesolithic ancestors are known along the east coast by their often-extensive kitchen-middens which were, in effect, prehistoric rubbish dumps. Workshops of these, and particularly of the subsequent Neolithic communities, are equally impressive in sheltered bays beneath the Chalk cliffs of Co. Antrim where there are large accumulations of reject flint flakes, while inland in the same county Neolithic factory sites such as the Tievebulliagh mountain screes exploited an exceptionally suitable stone for polished axes. The massive stone monuments (megaliths) in which the latest of these peoples buried their dead collectively are widespread and varied. More than a thousand remain as familiar landmarks on hilltops or on lower ground in all parts of the country: court cairns, gallery graves, passage graves, portal dolmens and wedge tombs, and they range into Bronze Age times. But of the pattern of agriculture which was introduced by these peoples and, indeed, of their settlements, the picture is only now starting to emerge. Bronze Age habitation sites are probably the small level clearings surrounded by circular placings of stone, and their burial mounds (tumuli), though generally small, are often gathered together in considerable cemeteries. Ritual sites, too, the 'Fairy Rings' (stone circles), alignments, and single pillar stones (gallauns) are plentiful and very well known. Even their mining centres are recognisable in a number of places, especially the large cluster of undisturbed workings high up on Mount Gabriel near Schull in West Cork.

From before the start of the Iron Age (c. 250 BC) and right through early Christian times there were circular field monuments which, apart from the high mountain areas, are ubiquitous today. Tens of thousands remain and some were inhabited as late as the 1600s. In the boulder clay lowlands these are the familiar ring forts: *rath*, *lios* and *dún* in Irish, which terms embrace a great many local place-names. These are commonly small, single-bank structures with an enclosing ditch and sometimes hut foundations, perhaps with an underground passage (souterrain) inside.

The most insignificant of these little monuments were, perhaps, simple stock enclosures, since it was necessary to pen farm animals nightly for safety against wolves and to prevent damage to the crops. Others, large and multivallate, were often the seats of important personages, for example Tara, which was the seat of the High Kings of Ireland. In the drumlin country of the Cavan region they were suitably sited on hill-tops, and there is also a group of major hill-forts, big enough to enclose a small farm in some cases, which were probably important habitation and ritual centres. Dún Ailinne in Kildare, Rathgall in Carlow, Brusselstown Ring in Wicklow and Emhain Macha (Navan Fort) in Armagh are examples.

Stone-walled enclosures (cashels) are largely their counterparts in the rocky areas, particularly conspicuous in Co. Clare and Co. Kerry. Again, some are trivial while others are imposing structures with internal wall-walks and an encircling, jumbled-stone *chevaux-de-frise*. Among the latter are Staigue, near Schull in Kerry, Grainán Aileach in Donegal and, of course, Dún Aengus and Dún Mór in the Aran Islands. Other contemporary fortifications are related differently to the local scene. In coastal areas promontory forts achieved their objective with a minimum of effort by a fosse and bank in earth or stone, cutting across the narrow neck of the promontory. The site of the Bailey Lighthouse at Howth, north of Dublin, is one of these, Dunbeg near Ventry in Kerry another.

In the marsh and lake regions of north-central Ireland especially, fortified islands (crannogs), natural or man-made on a foundation of stake-bound brushwood, were very numerous, either as permanent residences, such as the seventh century royal seat of the Kings of Meath at Lagore, or as safe refuges. All of these structures must represent a considerable population in parts of the Irish lowlands but, since agriculture has been continuous down to today, earthworks have been ploughed out in most places. Of the farms on which they centred little remains except for the fugitive crop marks locally visible from the air. On the lighter soils at higher levels there has been less disturbance and the old field walls can still be recognised widely, for instance at the royal centre of the west, Rathcroghan in Co. Roscommon.

Religious settlements of the early Christian church date from the sixth century and remain in hundreds of ruined sites all over Ireland. In many places these are hallowed ground still, and have been used for burials into modern times. The native church was monastic, with a strong eremitical flavour early on, and many of the oldest sites are in remote and almost inaccessible places, such as Skellig Michael off the Kerry coast, and the islands of Inishkea and Aran. The place-name 'Dysert' as in Dysert O'Dea in Clare shows that these bear analogy with the desert monasteries of the East and testify to the extreme austerity of the religious calling in early times. In the far-off Dingle peninsula many of these sites remain little disturbed today. Their remains are generally a stone-walled enclosure which has traces of beehive dwelling huts inside. Recumbent and standing cross-slabs mark burials of deceased members of the community and there is a small oratory or two, or a primitive church.

Some early sites connected with the saints became famous pilgrimage centres in Medieval times, such as St Kevin's, Glendalough, and St Patrick's Purgatory in Donegal. There are many holy wells throughout the country which are similarly honoured by celebrations on a parochial level on the local saint's feast day. By the tenth and eleventh centuries several centres had become large monastic towns, walled and with elaborate church buildings, and such striking features as round towers (used as belfries and as protection from raiders) and high crosses. They were, in fact, centres of art and learning whose reputation travelled far beyond our shores. Some of these are still graced by impressive ruins: Glendalough, Kells, Monasterboice, Castledermot, Clonmacnoise, while of other great teaching centres such as Clonard and Bangor very little remains. In fact the number and size of these establishments has only recently come to light from aerial observations.

5. Artificial Landscapes

An end to the native Church with its distinctive traditions came suddenly when, just before the middle of the twelfth century, foundations of the newly established monastic orders from the European mainland appeared. The Cistercians came first (these were the forerunners of the Norman invaders who followed fast on their heels) and later came the Augustinians, Dominicans and Franciscans. From this time the country quickly took on the predominantly artificial aspect which governs it today. Major developments were alien rather than traditional in their origin and, in later centuries, the native culture and life survived only at a low level among an increasingly impoverished peasantry.

These new abbeys and friaries were major enclosed communities, wealthily endowed, and generally sited in the more prosperous parts of the country, while simultaneously towns arose under the new order with secular bishoprics and a parochial organisation to minister to the needs of the public. In time, their daughter houses multiplied and extended throughout the land until the final Dissolution of the Monasteries about the middle of the sixteenth century. Today, their imposing ruins have an elegant if stereotyped pattern. They are set near a stream to provide fish on Fridays and to run a mill, they have regularly laid-out buildings enclosing a quadrangle with church, cloisters, refectory, dormitory and other assets, and they sometimes house the effigied tombs of their patrons: Mellifont in Louth, Jerpoint in Kilkenny, Dunbrody in Wexford, Boyle in Roscommon, Holycross in Tipperary, and so many others. These are an imposing part of the landscape all over Ireland and are gaunt reminders of a foreign tradition which extinguished the native culture but which has influenced radically the development of modern Ireland.

In the Medieval period few diocesan cathedrals were built as episcopal sees. St Canice's in Kilkenny and Cashel are examples, but more distinctive today are the smaller manorial and parish churches and these, chiefly in the English-ruled territories and built to an English pattern, established the style for much of the rural church architecture which survives into modern times. These parish churches were usually the site of the priest's residence and in the troubled days of Gaelic resurgence in the fourteenth century they were much in need of protection. The most striking feature is a massive square tower with upstairs levels having a fireplace and other provisions so as to serve as the priest's quarters. Its top floor provided the belfry and battlements to complete the resemblance to contemporary tower houses from which much of its character derives.

Newcastle in south-west county Dublin, a royal borough at the time, has an excellent fourteenth century parish church in its present Church of Ireland building. In north County Meath Rathmore's ruined fifteenth century manorial church in the same style was built by the Plunkett and ·Cruise families. At the Dissolution monasteries came into private hands as residences or were made to serve as Protestant churches (Baltinglass, Graiguenamanagh). Edward Moore occupied Mellifont, Bective was purchased by Andrew Wyse, and Tintern in Wexford went to Anthony Colclough whose family resided in it until a few years ago.

Everywhere, too, the legacy of the Norman conquest is to be seen throughout the land in its military structures and, to a minor degree in the east and south in domestic sites. Motte-and-bailey earthworks, which carried defensive palisades and wooden dwellings when in use, were the temporary fortifications of the first few years of the invasion and were usually formed by modifying a suitable natural feature. They soon gave way to stone-built castles with massive keeps and strong curtain walls of which the early-thirteenth century examples, de Lacy's castle in Trim and de Courcy's at Carrickfergus, are still impressive enough, even if they do not compare with the great creations of feudalism in England and on the mainland of Europe.

Numerous, though less conspicuous, are the rectangular earthworks which represent the farmsteads in the lowlands of the occupied territory of this and slightly later times. A traveller through the Normandy countryside today will recognise their familiar pattern of habitation, for their counterparts are still in use there: rectangular sites of a half acre or so, bounded by substantial water-filled ditches whose material has been used to build a low interior bank on which large trees grow. The dwelling-house and farm buildings are set amid a grassy orchard in which pigs run free.

Very familiar are those smaller examples of the fifteenth and sixteenth centuries: the single, square tower houses set in the corner of a somewhat insignificant bawn which has usually disappeared. These are scattered through the occupied lowlands in their hundreds, for the most part acting as fortified residences rather than with particular strategic significance. Some were built by local Irish rulers, such as the pretty little O'Maille castle at Rockfleet in Mayo, a seat of the famed Grainuaile, contemporary of Elizabeth I of England. Well-known larger keeps are Bunratty and Cregganowen in Clare, Blarney in Cork, Ross in Kerry, and Dunsoghly in Dublin, while the well-preserved Cahir Castle is a sixteenth century edifice.

A typical Medieval farming system was developed in Ireland (it may well have been an import by the Norman invaders) and remained in operation in the poorer districts until the last century. This was rundale, an open-field pattern of cultivation in which small plots belonging to each of several families lie scattered widely apart through the whole unfenced area under cultivation. Beyond it, livestock grazed freely in the common land, to be returned to an enclosure each night for safety. These plots were typically long and narrow strips, a nominal furlong in length, this being the distance a team of oxen could plough without resting. Where hand cultivation was employed, however, they might be more equidimensional in shape. Traces of rundale can be recognised widely in Donegal and the west. In poorer ground elsewhere their long furrowed plots are still occasionally delineated by the lines of cleared-off stones and, in places, modern field patterns may inherit their arrangement. In the poorer districts many commonages still function.

These rundale areas, which in a few places survived into the present century, were associated with small hamlets, the Irish clachans. These were clusters of cottages, each perhaps with its few outbuildings in a small haggard for penning stock, but lacking community facilities of any sort. The cottages themselves were traditional: single-storey, thatched, with two or three rooms in line, and rounded-off in appearance, which gives them a cosy look. In clay country they would be mud-walled, in rocky ground of stone, and with a whitewash finish for weather-proofing. This distinctive Irish cottage, which dates back at least to the 1700s, remains a familiar feature of the Irish landscape in many rural areas.

The picturesque fishing village of the Claddagh survived almost within the city limits of Galway into the 1930s, and one can still see traces of clachans with attendant rundale a short distance from Dublin, in the Glencullen Valley, for instance. The very common place-name of 'Bally' (from the Irish *báile*) often denotes such a hamlet.

In the uninhabited mountain lands transhumance was practised generally, as the term 'booleying', referred to in so many native townland names in these parts (Boleynass, 'the booley of the waterfall', Woodenboley, and many others) indicates. It was a seasonal operation in which the women and children encamped on the high pastures between spring and autumn with their flocks. The sites of these booleys are marked by many clusters of stone huts, now unroofed, on the banks of mountain streams in remote sheltered places.

The social gulf which separated the natives from the rising Ascendancy, composed in part of early Norman immigrants, but particularly of the settled planters of the sixteenth and seventeenth centuries, increased to become a total barrier. It reached its peak with the establishment by the latter of the great demesnes of Georgian times, their stately mansions set landscaped amidst spacious parklands, and supported by rents derived from the native tenants in the district around. The tall stone walls which run for miles to enclose them are a conspicuous feature, often the product of relief work in famine times, as also are the occasional conspicuous follies. Associated deer-parks and isolated patches of scrub as fox-coverts testify to the sporting pastimes of the day. In a number of the larger estates retainers were housed in neat villages nearby, which often have a distinctive architecture and uniform plan centering on a village square or mall, attractive in their setting yet totally foreign to the countryside in which they lie. Besides these estate towns, local businesses grew up at many centres as the island's population burgeoned in the 1700s so that, as well as essential services such as a smithy, there were mills based on convenient water power, and breweries, together with a church (Church of Ireland) and glebe house.

It will surprise many to find that the all-pervading pattern of lowland fields in Ireland is for the most part no more than two or three centuries old, as are their accompanying hedgerows. Our field systems of today came about chiefly by the enclosing operations of the 1700s and early 1800s when the landlord system largely developed among the Ascendancy land holders. The land was divided out by professional surveyors into a regular pattern of basically-rectangular fields with a general regard for the topographical aspects of the terrain. At these fertile levels they were typically large and spacious, while in the poor lands of swamp and mountain country the native inhabitants were left to fence off their fields, piecemeal perhaps, in a pattern of small, rounded-off enclosures.

In the clayey lowlands boundaries are characteristically of earthen banks and ditches, needed to carry off water. The former are covered with bushes such as hawthorn and briars, and sometimes lined with tall beech and ash which gives the country a deceptively wooded appearance in many places. In rocky districts, the limestone areas of Galway and Roscommon, the granite country of Mourne, and the sandstone uplands of the south-west, it is stone-wall terrain with the drainage ditches often unnecessary.

As country towns increased in population in the late 1700s a major communications network began to be established, highways which run direct from point to point with little regard to topography. These were apart from the multitude of minor bohereens which jink their way irregularly between adjacent farms. The era of canal building started about the same time but later halted with the onset of the railways which began in the 1830s. Land division meant, of course, a breakdown of the open-field rundale system and the clustered dwellings or clachans which it supported, so that in the last century the new farmhouses were conveniently situated on each farm and the disperse pattern of rural settlement which is so distinctive of modern Ireland quickly became established.

In Ireland, towns were an innovation of the Vikings just a thousand years ago when they established the first trading centres near major eastern and southern river-mouths: Dublin, Wicklow, Arklow, Wexford, Waterford, Cork and Limerick. Private housing conditions in these

43 *continued on page 60* ▶

Clew Bay, Co. Mayo

The broad basin of Clew Bay is a fold trough in Carboniferous Limestone which runs east and west. Our viewpoint is from the pilgrimage path up Croagh Patrick, Ireland's holy mountain, where the patron saint fasted in penance. It is, in fact, a much older religious centre, a Lughnasa station, where in pre-Christian times the Druids on Midsummer's Day performed their long-forgotten rites; now, christianised, it is celebrated at this time by tens of thousands of pilgrims.

Away to the north, warm-coloured Old Red Sandstone slopes down to the sea around Mallaranny, and on the foreshore of Rockfleet Bay stands the lovely little sixteenth-century tower house, Rockfleet Castle, of the O'Máille chieftainess, Granuaile, Elizabeth I's famous adversary. Its foundations are a flat, clayey limestone, the accumulation of a warm, muddy sea scattered with bun-shaped colonies of corals and fungus-like algal growths which, with many other fossils present, appear as they lived on

the sea-floor 300 million years ago.

The limestone supports a belt of fertile farmland but, sub-surface, it is riddled with solution channels. The surface cover is boulder clay moulded into smooth oval hills by passage of the ice-sheets over them, and they form a conspicuous drumlin belt which passes out into the bay as the 'Thousand Islands'. My father-in-law, who lived in these parts, told me that he went one Sunday to the little church of Kilmeena, tucked away amid these hills well inland to the east, to seek one James Gill. The shop-keeper whom he asked immediately walked across the room to look fixedly out the back window. 'Yes', he said, 'he'll be at Mass today.' The little pond at the end of his garden was dry and this provided the answer. Connected via the honeycombed limestone it rose and fell with the tide. He saw that the tide was out: James would have driven over from his island.

The Donegal Mountains

This view north from the crest of the granite Derryveagh mountains is one of the most impressive inland panoramas in Donegal. In the distance the pyramidal peak of Errigal dominates, at nearly 2,500 feet one of the county's highest summits. With its characteristic profile it lies at the south-western end of the great quartzite ridge, which includes the comparable profiles of Aghla and Muckish. One has a glimpse of the little village of Dunlewy on its west side whose ruined church was built from the local sugary white marble, an outcrop of which stretches away in the low ground to the north-east beneath the quartzite.

The Poisoned Glen, celebrated among botanists as the haunt of uncommon plants, occupies the main foreground. Its broad U-shape shows that it was much enlarged and deepened by a glacier which took off at the precipitous lip immediately before us from its feeding ground in the Derryveagh snowfields. On the flattened valley floor a little stream meanders sluggishly out of sight over the broad expanse of peaty moorland.

The great expanse of Derryveagh granite which forms this mountain backbone was injected along a major movement zone in the crystalline metamorphic rocks of the region, during a period of earth deformation which we call Caledonian, about 400 million years ago. It was this which developed the structure and rock characteristics throughout the Scottish Highlands, Donegal and Mayo. All these features evolved deep in the earth's crust, but since then long-continued erosion has laid them bare at the surface, and today their characters dominate the topography of Donegal.

Benmore Head, Co. Kerry

In the remote south-west of Ireland the shepherd and his dog are a familiar part of the scene, where mountain sheep are a basic source of wealth and Gaelic is still a living tongue. This, the Dingle peninsula, was a favourite retreat of the hermits of the early Christian church. Until recently more than a hundred of their little beehive huts (clocháns) were scattered through the Fahan district alone, and the region has scores of monastic sites, oratories, ogham stones, cross-slabs and later church remains. The number which now survives is, alas, drastically reduced, yet the tradition of building circular, corbelled stone huts for outbuildings is alive still. At its narrowest point a ditch-and-bank transects the headland, enclosing a large area of its apex, one of the many promontory forts. Some of these are emphatic fortifications; others, such as this one, perhaps, may be simple stock enclosures.

South-east Ireland's coastline comprises a series of mountain-

ous promontories, each a big sandstone fold arch, which alternate with deep-going inlets sited on the intervening fold troughs. Benmore Head terminates one of the former, extended seawards in the group of offshore islands known as the Blaskets. It is the furthest reach of continental Europe; the fold belt here stops abruptly at the ocean. A remarkable discovery in modern geology is that the Atlantic is a relatively young terrestrial feature, initiated roughly 150 million years ago by the spreading apart from a central rift (now the Mid-Atlantic Ridge) of the Old and New World continents which, till then, formed a single unit. Identical structures and rock formations match up on either side of the ocean. We find the continuations of Kerry's mountains in Newfoundland and Nova Scotia, and North America still recedes from us by about one centimetre per year.

The Central Lowlands

This view of the east Galway countryside is obtained not far from the city on the way to Oughterard, at a point where the Central Lowlands of Ireland come against the old granite and crystalline massif of Connemara. It ranges over lush grassy fields in the flat limestone country to the extensive solution lake of Corrib in the distance. Here and there the pretty little whitewashed cottages of a purely agricultural population are scattered far apart. The fields are small, as are the farm holdings. Sheep are the principal livestock and potatoes are always grown. The predominant stone walls add a very distinctive touch to the landscape of this part of the country (Galway east and Roscommon), their purpose as much to take up the loose stones as to form enclosures. No

ditches are needed since, beneath the light soil, cavernous limestone soaks up surface water.

Hawthorn bushes are profuse along the walls and give a
luxuriant aspect to the countryside but they are virtually the
biggest trees in view. Around the beginning of May their blossom
engulfs the landscape, a magnificent sight, especially near Kinvarra
in the south of the county. No wonder the ancient druidical feast
of Bealtaine, which celebrated the first of May, was such a major
event in the Celtic calendar, probably related to the widespread
resurrection rituals which pervaded the early religions of the
Near East.

Killarney Lakes

Killarney's verdant and magnificent setting is a blend of geology, geography and climate. Fold ranges of Old Red Sandstone, forming Ireland's highest mountains, reach 3,414 feet in Carrantuohill nearby. The low ground is Carboniferous Limestone. The region has the highest rainfall, and the Atlantic Gulf Stream warms it, producing mild conditions the year round. Muckross Lake, like Lough Leane, is essentially a solution depression in the limestone of which ragged skerries are relics. Immediately in view, the Colleen Bawn Rock was so named in recent times for the tragic beauty whose fate inspired Benedict's opera *The Lily of Killarney*. Underfoot, the path is made from waste of the old Muckross mines. They were worked in prehistoric times (sandstone mauls can still be picked out of the debris) and more recently by the Herbert family to whom the notorious Raspe was advisor. He died in 1794 and his remains lie in the hill-top cemetery a few

miles to the east.

Its natural circumstances ensure that Killarney holds much interesting natural history. Ireland's oldest National Park here embraces the largest of its native oak woods. Evergreen arbutus and holly are lower canopy members of this forest whose ground flora abounds in ferns, liverworts and mosses. In fact, three-fourths of all the moss species in the country are recorded here. The little Killarney fern (*Trichomanes*) is at home in the spray of its waterfalls, and royal fern flourishes as nowhere else. Ireland's sole native herd of red deer inhabits the woods and uplands. Even the lakes have their distinctive inhabitants. The Killarney shad is a unique form (*Killarniensis*) of one of the marine herring family which migrates into estuaries to breed. It seems to have been cut off in a former marine extension here and has since developed into a purely freshwater creature with its own characteristics.

Lough Derg and the Shannon

Ireland's premier river, 240 miles long from its appearance in the Shannon Pot resurgence in Cavan, has a peculiar course. The initial, longest stretch across the Central Lowlands is a broad, wandering river which swells imperceptibly into a string of lakes: Allen, Ree, Derg. At the mouth of the latter it suddenly changes character, narrowing abruptly, while the gradient steepens in the (former) Killaloe rapids. The drop, over one hundred feet, served to locate Ireland's first hydroelectric generator hereabouts in 1925. In fact, the big river is constrained in a narrow gap while breaking through the old slate massif of the Arra mountains in Tipperary, which continues as Slieve Bernagh on the Clare side.

Rivers coursing across mountain ranges are anomalous. The likely explanation is that millions of years ago young Chalk formation, tilted southwards, lay over southern Ireland, and on its high surface the ancient Shannon flowed. As denudation slowly re-

moved the Chalk, the river bit by bit cut down its channel. Eventually the hidden slates and Carboniferous Limestone emerged to daylight while the Chalk disappeared completely. The river, set in its course, continued across them as the altogether different land surface of today was revealed. Hidden remnants of this postulated Chalk have been found in Kerry recently and indestructible flints from it are scattered over the region generally.

This view across Lough Derg, just above the narrows, is from near Portroe. The limestone plain, spread with glacial deposits, supports prosperous farms with their rectangular pattern of large fields. The lake shore has a fringe of planted hardwood with much the same aspect as the natural woodland which dominated the scene in olden times.

Lowland Bog, Co. Longford

The topography of central Ireland is such that when the icesheets disappeared the entire middle reaches of the Shannon were a great shallow lake, many times the area of Lough Neagh. Its lime-rich surrounds supported a rush-and-sedge vegetation which formed fen peats encroaching into the water. When this reached a foot or two thickness it sealed off the soil nutriments below and the swamp vegetation abruptly changed in character. Bog mosses in particular began to flourish, as did plants suited to the increasingly acid conditions. The moss has the ability to swell with water like a sponge, and so the bog surface became gently arched above the surrounding lands.

This is the raised bog of the Irish lowlands, its surface diversifed by hummocks of bog moss with pools trapped among them. Bog cotton, deer grass and insectiverous plants – sundew and butterwort – characterise the harsh environment. Where it has dried out, heathers, namely ling and erica, cover the firmer

ground. This dried-out bog near Roosky, with turf-cutting in the old-fashioned, manual way, shows a layered character arising from the fact that peat formation (humification or breakdown of the vegetable remains) is a function of climate. Warm, dry conditions make for structureless, homogeneous peat; cool, wet climates favour preservation of raw plant debris.

Airborne pollen falling on the surface is minutely preserved in the peat as the bog builds up in time. Individual grains, especially tree pollen, are clearly identifiable, and their changing abundances at successive levels enable the forest composition and its variation to be followed over the 9,000 years since peat formation began. Pine forest, a taiga vegetation, predominated at first but gave way to deciduous woodland as climate improved. Pine became extinct by 1,500 BC, and the conifers now growing are reintroductions.

The Ben Bulben Plateau

A panoramic view of the north-western border of a spectacular tableland region, where the abrupt, prow-like profile of Ben Bulben forms its edge. Table mountain landscape dominates an area not far short of 1,000 square miles in counties Sligo, Leitrim and Mayo. In it flat beds of Carboniferous Limestone, tilted very gently eastwards, have been dissected by deep-cut valleys into a series of separate, flat-topped plateaux. Because of the tilt, the limestone formation gives way eastwards to overlying sandstones, but the general morphological aspect of the plateau landscape is similar in each case. Vertical fractures (joints) control the upright cliff faces, skirted lower down by a more gently-sloping scree of boulders which have fallen away in the course of time.

The rock formations and their disposition are as in the Moher region of Co. Clare, and the landscape which developed has much in common with the latter.

The limestone cliff habitat has many unusual calcicole plants, and the plateau above has some notable arctic relics, probably survivals of the tundra vegetation that first colonised the land after the ice-sheets disappeared 10,000 years ago: alpine saxifrage, mountain aven and others. Our view faces southwards from the N15 across gently undulating lowland in glacial deposits. Its minor rises are reclaimed farmland with scattered homesteads, each in its shelter belt of trees, while bog fills the ill-drained depressions among them.

early urban settlements were crowded and squalid. Later there were Norman towns associated with the major castles and abbeys: Kildare, Trim, Galway; and there are many subsequent Plantation towns such as Derry, Portlaoise (Maryborough), Mallow, Gorey, Fermoy. Small Georgian estate towns were connected with some of the demesnes of Ascendency families: Adare (Wyndham-Quin), Strokestown (Mahon), Birr (Parsons), Westport (Browne) and many others.

Towns which developed last century, following the opening-up of communications and industry, were Belfast (the single outstanding instance of rapid growth in a great city) and smaller places such as Portlaw and Lisburn, based on cotton and linen industries respectively, the first established by Quaker immigrants, the Malcomsons. Market towns often have the simplest of plans: a single line of houses and shops extending on each side of the main road which is greatly broadened to serve as a suitable venue for the market. In some instances they carry the name of Stradbally (from the Irish *sráid báile*, street town). In the last decade or so satellite towns have begun to crowd around major cities: Tallaght, Ballyfermot and Blanchardstown in Dublin, for example.

The amenities of these large population centres include cathedrals (normally the seats of secular bishops) such as Christchurch and St Patrick's in Dublin, and St Canice's in Kilkenny which go back to Norman times. The old town walls have largely been demolished or swallowed up during the expansion from the eighteenth century to date. Apart from Athenry and the early seventeenth century example in Derry none dominate the modern town plans, though a few impressive gateways remain: St Laurence's in Drogheda, for example. There are also the impressive military barracks, typically star-shaped and dating from the seventeenth to nineteenth centuries. Some were occupied until fairly recently, for example Charles Fort, Kinsale (built 1677). Others, such as James Fort nearby (c. 1601) are long in ruins. Still others, such as the nineteenth century Spike Island, have now a different use. Among the latter structures, most prominent of all are the little pepper-pot fortifications in granite, called martello towers from the Corsican prototype, which were hurriedly erected in Napoleonic times to frustrate an invasion that never materialised.

Abandoned mines of modern times (Tynagh, near Loughrea, for example) are conspicuous eyesores with their derelict buildings, great waste heaps and scars of opencast working, unless care has been taken to rehabilitate the land, and this also applies to quarries. Those of olden times, however, have mellowed and blend picturesquely with the landscape. They are now instructive as to how such operations were carried out in the early years of the industrial era. The hundred years around 1800 were the heyday of historical Irish mining when Ireland was a major producer of copper and other base metals.

In the Avoca Valley of Wicklow an extensive belt of copper-iron mineralisation has been worked continuously from Medieval times. Old engine houses at the head of the shafts dot the countryside and south of the valley, where reckless past workings honeycombed the ground, is the spectacular collapse which occurred in the 1840s, with no loss of life, fortunately, since it was St Patrick's Day and the miners were drowning their shamrock in the town. Further west, the remote valleys of Glendalough, Glenmalure and Glendasan have lead-zinc workings in the granite mountains while at the north, overlooking Dublin city, Ballycorus still features its shot towers and its gigantic brick flue winding up the hillside to remove noxious zinc fumes. The buildings lower down held triphammers and other ore-dressing equipment (they are now converted into a modern factory) and, till recently, the millpond which supplied motive power completed the ensemble.

In Ulster, Newtownards worked lead, as did Clontibret in Monaghan. The latter also produced antimony. On the Waterford coast Bunmahon copper mines were of major importance, as were Allihies and Goleen in West Cork, though it is said that many of the workings here were 'salted' to attract prospective, if undiscriminating, investors. Near Killarney, the Ross Island mines were worked in antiquity, and during the eighteenth century the infamous Raspe, famed as the creator of Baron Munchausen, acted as advisor to the mine owners and first noticed the purple cobalt bloom which was then being jettisoned in the lake.

In later times, the seventeenth century chiefly, for that is when England's oakwoods were exhausted, iron smelting moved to seek the charcoal sources still available in this country for a short time longer. Bloomeries operated great sod-covered mounds, alternating crushed ore and charcoal, through which an air blast was forced to reduce the iron to a spongy mass. Places named Furnace (in Wicklow's Vale of Clara and beyond Newport in Mayo, for example) mark their sites which are of necessity beside a stream to supply water power to the crushing hammers, and have waste heaps of iron slag and charcoal. Inconspicuous in our landscape today they nonetheless played a significant role in the Irish landscape, for their enormous demands on fuel sounded the deathknell of the last of our native timber.

The last century has contributed many features to today's towns and cities: railway stations, factories, port installations and the varied public institutions which embrace schools, hospitals, courthouses, local government offices, and so on. It is, however, the twentieth century whose effects now predominate and produce the awesome suburban sprawl of our greater conurbations, with their industrial estates, satellite dormitories, airports, and radiating lines of communication, energy transmission and the rest, which like fungal mycelia bid fair to engulf the entire surroundings.

The short period since World War II has altered our rural landscape even more radically than the two centuries that went before, and while the changes make for efficiency in modern terms they are scarcely pleasing to the eye: consolidated large fields for mechanised farming, wire fences bare of hedges, extensive corrugated iron farm buildings, stereotyped cottages and great ribbons of evenly-graded highway traversing the landscape where, nevertheless, the abandoned buildings of older times remain in ruin as eyesores. Exotic softwood plantations now cover great areas of mountain land. They represent a valuable if monotonous asset, and they are matched lower down, in their sterile aspect, by the hundreds of acres of bare, cutaway bog which do not.

Compared with most of Europe Ireland still has major areas in an unspoilt natural state, however, and the varied beauty of its panoramas is largely unimpaired. Despite modern pressures a great deal remains to be saved for the enjoyment of future generations. The case for its protection will best be served today if we appreciate the significance of our landscape's features and their long history.

6. Place and Family Names

Place-names are an illuminating facet of the local scene. Most of those which grace our maps go back four or five centuries and many date to pre-Conquest times. Some, in fact, belong to the Iron Age and a few may relate to the first Celtic tribes to colonise Ireland in the centuries before the start of the Christian era. The Dumnonii from south-west Britain may have been the invading group who set up such royal sites as the hill-forts of Tara and Dún Ailinne, and Maynooth (from the Gaelic *Mag Nuadat*, 'the plain of Nuadu') is believed to refer to the Celtic god Nodens of classical Roman authors. Possibly the Brigantes from northern Britain immigrated to become a major Leinster tribe, Uí Bairrche (from *Uí*, 'descendants of'), who have left their name as the Bargy barony in Wexford.

In Celtic Ireland territory was named after the tribe which inhabited it, and tribes, in turn, were usually named from the founder or head of the chief family. So we have such names as Offaly from Uí Failge and, in Carlow, the baronies of Idrone from the Celtic tribe of Uí Dróna. There are also, for example, Tyrone (*Tír Eoghan*, 'the land of Eoghan') and Shelmalier barony in Wexford (from *Síl*, 'the seed or descendants of', Maeluidir).

The place-names of early Christian times make reference particularly to foundations associated with the pioneering monks in the sixth and seventh centuries. Though their wooden buildings have long gone there is an abundance of these sites throughout the country. Templepatrick in Antrim is from St Patrick himself. St Mullins in Carlow is *Teach Molaing*, 'the house of St Molaing'. The many Kilbrides (*Cill Brighid*, 'St Bridget's church') are related to Bridget the sixth century abbess of Kildare. Kilkenny (St Canice's church), Kilmallock (St Mocheallogh's church), Monasterboice (Buite's monastery) are others. The last named is from the Latin which was introduced at this time and 'Dysert', for example, refers to the desolate setting of Kiladysart and Dysart O'Dea in Clare. *Cluain*, a meadow, often a water meadow as at Clonmacnoise, reflects the fact that many were sited in marshes, or on little raised clearings in the bogs of the Central Lowlands as is the remotely beautiful Monainche ('the bog island') near Roscrea.

In the ninth and tenth centuries Viking names are introduced, particularly for coastal features along the east, e.g. Carlingford, Skerries (meaning a reef) and Ireland's Eye (Islet), while Wexford, Wicklow (Wykyngelo, *lo* being the Viking word used for a water meadow or marsh) and Arklow tell us that these, the first towns in Ireland, were also Viking creations foreign to the native way of life. The north Dublin territory of Fingal likewise refers to these fair-haired foreigners (from the Gaelic, *Fionn Ghall*).

From Norman times (the twelfth and thirteenth centuries) come many place-names in the lands taken over by the conquerors. Brittas, as in Brittas Bay, Co. Wicklow, is the wooden palisade (*bretasche*) erected as a defence by the newcomers, and Moate in Co. Longford refers to the motte-and-bailey fortifications which mark the first years of the Conquest. Borris (from the Gaelic *burghis*) as in Burrisoole, Co. Mayo and other places, refers to the lots of land let out to the burgesses or freemen of Norman towns. 'Manor' and 'Grange', the latter referring to out-farms associated with monasteries, are likewise common. Many townland names mark family holdings, for the new-comers found it convenient to replace the existing Gaelic by, for example, Dollardstown and Painestown in Co. Meath, which refer to historical figures, Freynestown and Davidstown in west Wicklow, and so on.

The Gaelic *dún, rath, lios* (as in Lismore, 'the big lios'), now effectively synonymous, derive from residential sites and attach themselves to thousands of places throughout the country where an earthwork of the type of a ring fort is involved. Conversely in rocky terrain, the distinctive stone-built counterpart (cashel) will be found to substi-tute. Many of the structures are now long demolished, for the sites were convenient for later habitations. Some of these, no doubt, are early as, for instance, Dunsany (*Dun Saithne*) in Meath, referring to a Celtic tribe, but most are of indefinite age and several were occupied down to a few centuries ago. It seems likely, too, that the Irish *Báile* represented in thousands of townland and village names applies to hamlets of Medieval and later times. Ballyshane near Shillelagh in Wicklow, for instance, is named from one Shane O'Byrne who left the district in 1542.

But Irish place-names, especially in the wilder, less populous, regions, often relate to natural features and cannot be closely dated. Esker in Co. Dublin is one of several places with this name, going back at least to Nor-man times, and drumlin, with *Druim* ('a back') is likewise a component in many place-names. Both have passed into international usage to describe these glacial features: dis-tinctive raised gravel ridges in the first case and, in the second, oval boulder-clay hillocks such as occur in their thousands across north-central Ireland. Those ephemeral lakes (turloughs) are also an Irish speciality and name several places in the limestone regions of the west. The widespread use of Derry (*Doire*, 'an oak wood'), *Cuillin* (holly) and also *Fuinséog* (ash) as in Ballyfunshoge and *Áirne* (sloe) in Killarney, refer to the great mixed-decidu-ous forest which was once the natural vegetation of the Irish lowlands. Other place-names recall long gone members of our fauna, for example Kanturk ('the boar's head') and Seskinamadra ('the marsh of the wolf') in Co. Limerick.

An Irish resurgence followed the spectacularly successful invasion of the Normans in the fourteenth and fifteenth centuries, a time when the new settlers were forced to consolidate their gains into more restricted territories. To this period belongs such geographical terms as Joyce's Country, still used to refer to this family's lands in north Galway, Dillon's Country in Westmeath, Archbold's Country around Bray, and others. About this time, too, many Norman names were gaelicised, such as Ballyvaltron and Ballylaffin in Wicklow, settled by the Waldrons and Laffans respectively. When Henry VIII inaugurated the Kingship of Ireland it gave rise to a new breed of English immigrant to fill the many administrative posts so created. Several of these possessed themselves of large country estates whose townland names today tell the tale: Binghamstown on the Mullet peninsula where Sir Richard Bingham, president of Connaught in 1584, settled down; Bagnelstown in Carlow from Elizabeth's marshal; Cootehill in Cavan obtained by Sir Charles Coote in the seventeenth century. Townlands with the name Collegeland would refer to dispossessed lands given to Trinity College, Dublin.

The first systematic plantations of English settlers, by William and Mary in the middle of the sixteenth century, saw counties Laois and Offaly renamed Queen's County and King's County, with the plantation towns Maryborough and Philipstown respectively. These have only recently returned to their original Gaelic names. A half-century later in the Ulster Plantation of James I Derry town correspondingly acquired the prefix 'London' with reference to the origin of its new undertakers, and later on Charleville in Cork was named to honour Charles II. In more peaceful circumstances immigrants came from the Rhenish Palatinate in 1709 to two districts: south-east Limerick and north-east Carlow, to strengthen the local economy. These have long been absorbed yet the operation is still recalled by the place-name Palatine in each of these districts.

Most place-names were already established by the seventeenth century and those of more recent origin are in English, for Gaelic was now out of general use: Oldcastle in Meath, Waterville in Kerry, Ashford in Wicklow and Westport (a demesne town of the Marquis of Sligo) are examples. Archbishop Boyle, when he acquired the town of Ballycomyn in Wicklow (earlier Villa Comyn, the medieval estate granted to the first Norman Archbishop of Dublin) renamed it with the modern Blessington in 1669. In the north many new names arrive with the planters from lowland Scotland: Crawfordsburn, Draperstown, Newtownhamilton, Scotstown. Saundersgrove in Wicklow is a much later (1709) example of the same type established by the descendants of a Cromwellian officer while others (the many Deerpark townlands are examples) were created by the landed gentry on their eighteenth and nineteenth century demesnes. Some peculiarly reflect their cultural aspirations or experiences on the Grand Tour: Delphi in Mayo, Valclusa near Enniskerry in Wicklow, Mount Venus in south Dublin. Others named their estates for themselves: French Park, Loftus Hall, Moore Park; or for their wives: Annesgrove, Mount Juliet, Bessbrook.

Family names, in a way, play a comparable role in the Irish countryside to those of places, for the multitudes of different family groups spread through various parts of our country also reflects its complex history. Their form became permanently established around the eleventh and twelfth centuries with 'Ó' and 'Mac' referring to 'descent from' and 'son of' respectively in Gaelic names, though these were often dropped later on as part of an anglicisation process. Likewise there are the Norman prefixes 'Fitz', equivalent to 'Mac', and 'de' though the latter most often denotes the region from which the family emanated. Some modern names were those of important chieftains, (*Rí*, or local kings) of Celtic and early Christian times: O'Conor, O'Neill, O'Donnell, O'Rourke, O'More, O'Brien, MacCarthy. Others are Norman, such as the Fitzgeralds who accompanied Strongbow with the first groups of invaders, and the de Burghs and Butlers who came shortly after with Prince John. The latter are descendants of Theobald Walter ('le boteler') who served as his butler.

These names are widespread today but, on the whole, farming people, unless forcibly dispossessed, tend to cling to their traditional territories over the centuries. It is not surprising that the poor and remote terrain of west Kerry and west Cork respectively are still the O'Sullivan and O'Driscoll homelands, or that O'Dohertys dominate in Inishowen, but in spite of dispossession from their traditional lands in the richer midlands, O'Reillys, Duffys and

O'Farrells are still plentiful there, as are Kavanaghs and Kinsellas in the south-east. O'Tooles and O'Byrnes maintained the old Irish lifestyles and customs in the hill regions of east Wicklow well into the seventeenth century. Many are still there, while along the coast of the country are those Viking descendants the Doyles (from the Gaelic *Dubh Gall*, 'dark foreigner'). The Sweetmans are of like ancestry (literally *Swaitmen* 'the man of the black spear').

Gaelic tribes from Scotland emigrated to the north-east in Medieval times as mercenary soldiers: the gallowglass (*Gall Oglach*, 'foreign troops'). Of these there are the MacDonnells in the Glens of Antrim, and the MacSweeneys in Donegal. Even as far south as Cavan the MacCabes performed the same services for O'Rourke, and their descendants are numerous there.

From a foothold in Wexford in 1169 the Normans quickly spread to dominate nearly all the fertile lowlands of the country. De Lacy's knights divided up the ancient Kingdom of Meath and many of their families are still rooted there: Plunketts, the family of the Lords Fingal and Dunsany, Dillons, Nugents (*de Nogent*), Tuites, Tyrrells. The foot soldiers of the first invaders were mostly Flemings from Wales, but initially from Flanders, and they settled densely in the south of Wexford where their customs and Medieval Low Dutch dialect survived into the last century. These are the still-predominant Roches (from Rouse, near Haverfordwest in Wales), Devereux (from Normandy), Synnotts, Staffords. Graces, Purcells, Forrestals, Shortalls are families in the Nore and Barrow valleys while lower down the Suir were the seats of Powers and Tobins, the latter a gaelicisation of de St Aubyn. The Barry (*de Barri*) family shortly became established in Cork, while de Burgh, now mostly Burkes, later made wide conquests mostly in Connaught, followed there by Joyces from Wales. The latter predominate now in the Joyce Country along with Stauntons (probably from Stainton near Rouse) and others. In Ulster, families such as Seagrave and Whyte settled eastern Down at the expense of Irish such as MacGuinness and MacCartan.

Scarcely a century had passed before gaelicisation of many of these is noticeable, 'more Irish than the Irish themselves', as the saying went. In the old territory of the Route, roughly the Antrim side of the lower Bann, de Mandevilles became the Irish MacUidhilin in about 1270 after one Hugolin, the MacQuillins of this region today. A branch of the de Angulos living in Westmeath, from Gilbert, son of Jocelyn, became gaelicised as MacGoisdelbh about the same time. This later was corrupted to the well-known Costello which now names, in addition, a barony in east Mayo and the picturesque Costelloe village in Connemara.

Later English families arrived as government officials, ecclesiastics and so on to put down roots in north Kildare: Wogan, justiciar in the early fourteenth century, the Elizabethan clergymen Loftus and Boyle (though a majority of the Irish Boyles must derive from the Donegal clan of O'Baoighill). From the seventeenth century onwards Scottish planters arrived in Ulster in considerable numbers: Cunningham, Graham, Craig, Murray, Kyle and many others. Their names are still commonplace there, and at about the same time Jamesons, the well-known whiskey family, came to Dublin from Clackmannan.

One may wonder what it is that has produced the special quality of the Irish scene. Much of our country still has its basis in the ancient culture and, in its small area, a combination of varied natural features and the complicated record of human history gives it a great deal of variety. The well-known folklorist Seamus Delargy would often recall that Ireland had the oldest civilisation in Europe. The invaders, too, centuries after the Conquest, could still accept this when it suited them. That 'Europe was from old divided into four empires or *regna*, that of Rome, that of Constantinople, that of Ireland and that of Spain' was recalled by the English representative at the Council for Church Reform in Constance (1415).

Medieval Ireland was, in fact, the surviving outpost of the old Celtic race which had earlier dominated Europe. The Norman invasion and its sequel represent the stuggle for survival of this distinctive way of life against that of the new feudal Europe. Celtic lifestyle based itself ultimately on that of the Eurasian steppe nomads three or four thousand years ago, a pastoral economy which allowed a high degree of mobility; and the Celts in Ireland lived in widely-scattered, dispersed settlements. Their society and its government was organised on a tribal pattern based on the extended family or clan, which chose its rulers by popular acclaim. Land belonged to the tribe and conquests were to gain wealth, namely cattle, rather than to acquire territory. Its art was attractive and sophisticated but essentially unorganised: abstract and curvilinear rather than symetrical; fantastic, not realistic.

At the time of the Conquest Irish tribes were still mobile.

The O'Tooles and O'Byrnes, displaced east from their rich Kildare lands by Strongbow, could migrate to the mountain fastnesses and continue to operate according to their ancient customs and Brehon laws well into the seventeenth century. Individuals had grazing rights on the tribal lands, and this ancient custom today measures a farmer's holding on our hill commonages in so many collops, each the grazing of a single cow.

A century ago most counties had native speakers for whom Gaelic was their first tongue, and the language was in daily use even within sight of the capital city. We have Gaeltachts surviving in the far west, north and south and, harking back to the Druids, the Lughnasa festival is remembered with bonfires and pilgrimages on Irish hilltops still. Celtic settlement focussed on circular habitations: raths, cashels, crannogs, and the barren limestone plateaux of Clare and Aran show examples of how their field enclosures spread around these in shapeless fashion. When Christianity arrived, its monasteries, with the little beehive dwellings of the monks, directly follow this plan, and the distinctive Celtic church developed its organisation within the native tribal framework rather than attached to the universal church. These enclosures are in the same genre as the temporary stock pens of nomadic peoples. This is also the case with the sheep folds which are still erected in Ireland's hills, and the little stone-walled fields which encroach on the bare mountainsides in Kerry and Wicklow. In the well-rounded thatched cottages which constitute our characteristic vernacular architecture there is a similar inspiration. It is not, of course, that these follow a continuous tradition over the millennia; rather the widely separated generations have found analogous solutions to the same problems.

In Medieval times the Celtic peoples had a much less efficient organisation than that of their feudal neighbours, which was militarily the most effective in Europe. It suited the Norman invaders to denigrate totally the customs and manners, both secular and religious, of the Celtic culture with which they had no wish to find common ground. The astounding pace of the conquest reflects the impact of this aggressive new society on an old conservative civilisation which little understood the implications of territorial acquisition. Since land belonged to the tribe and not to its ruler, to the Irish *Rí* submission meant simply the temporary acceptance of an overlord rather than a permanent loss of territory. The people were easily persuaded, too, to welcome the new religious practices without realising that these, associating ecclesiatical and temporal power, were an intrinsic part of the new feudalism. Only this explains the magnitude of the native debacle; it also explains the on-going reaction which followed it and which saw in the twentieth century the emergence of the new Irish nation.

These two very distinctive cultures have coursed strongly through our nation in the succeeding ages, and Ireland is a land of several traditions which are not by any means perfectly assimilated. Their varied strands, which range from far beyond the limits of history right down to the present day, intermingle in the Irish scene and give it an interest all of its own.

Glossary

Algal Growths Aquatic plants which form a mat-like covering over reefs and are often preserved in *sedimentary rocks*.

Basalt A dark, fine-grained lava formed by the solidification of molten igneous *magma*.

Bedding Refers to the layers often present in sedimentary rocks (also known as *stratification*). A bedding plane is the surface separating one layer from another.

Boulder Clay The mass of glacial deposits left after the retreat of *glaciers* and ice-sheets; unsorted material containing everything from clay to boulders. Also known as drift.

Caledonian Deformation phase in the earth's history from 470 to 370 million years ago which led to the development of the chief mountain ranges of Leinster, Connaught and Ulster, of the Scottish Highlands, etc.

Carboniferous Geological period which began approximately 345 million years ago and lasted for about 65 million years.

Central Rift *See Mid-Atlantic Ridge.*

Dalradian A series of *sedimentary rocks*, now largely metamorphic, which formed between 800 and 500 million years ago in the Scottish Highlands (the ancient territory of Dal Riada) and range through northern and western Ireland.

Dolerite A medium-grained igneous rock similar to *basalt*.

Drift *See Boulder Clay.*

Drumlin Smooth, elongated *boulder clay* hill formed by the moulding action of a glacier on newly deposited morainic material.

Esker Winding gravel ridge deposited by a stream flowing underneath a *glacier* or discharging at its front.

Fault A fracture in the earth's crust along which movement, often extensive, has taken place.

Felspar (Feldspar) Common *silicate* mineral of aluminium, with potassium, sodium or calcium.

Flood Plain Flat deposits of sand and gravel formed when a river overflows its banks and covers the adjacent ground, producing a fertile tract of land.

Foraminifera Microscopic unicellular organisms, most of which have shells composed of calcium carbonate.

Glacier A mass of moving ice which moves slowly downwards under the force of gravity, either as an expansive ice-sheet or confined within valleys (valley glaciers).

Gneiss Coarse-grained *metamorphic rock* exhibiting a banded structure.

Gryke Solution fissure on the surface of Limestone formed by rain water containing carbon dioxide from the atmosphere.

Ice Age Phase in the earth's history when ice-sheets covered large areas of the earth. The last one ended about 10,000 years ago.

Igneous Rock Formed by solidification of molten *magma* on cooling.

Joints Fractures which traverse rocks without displacement (c.f. *faults*).

Lias Clay Geological formation beginning around 195 million years ago and lasting 15 million years.

Magma Molten rock material which forms *igneous rocks* on cooling.

Metamorphic Rock Rocks whose original character have been changed by recrystallisation due to high temperature, pressure, etc.

Micas *Silicate* minerals with aluminium, also potassium, iron, magnesium with sheet-like crystal structure and form.

Mid-Atlantic Ridge A major elevated feature of the Atlantic floor produced by repeated fracturing and pulling apart of the earth's crust.

Moraine Glacial feature composed of *boulder clay* deposited beneath the glacier as ground moraine, or at the ice front as a crescentic or terminal moraine.

Nunatak Isolated mountain peak projecting island-like through an ice-sheet.

O.D. 'Ordnance Datum', the zero level with reference to which altitudes of the land surface are determined.

Old Red Sandstone Sandstone formation accumulated between 390 and 345 million years ago.

Pegmatite Igneous rock with extremely large crystals, more than an inch across.

Peneplain Extensive area of low relief and elevation produced by long period of erosion.

Quartz Silicon dioxide mineral common in many rocks and veins.

Quartzite Hard, white metamorphic rock formed from a quartz-rich sandstone.

Schist Coarse-grained *metamorphic rock* with a parallel arrangement of its principal minerals.

Sedimentary Rock Formed by accumulation of detritus transported by water, wind or ice or by precipitation from solution (e.g. limestones).

Slaty Cleavage Plane of breakage which develops in fine-grained rocks as a result of intense deformation.

Silicates The most common rock-forming minerals, having silicon and oxygen as essential elements.

Stratification *See Bedding.*

Swallow Hole Surface depression in a limestone region through which a stream enters an underground drainage system.

Tertiary Geological era which began 65 million years ago and ended 2 million years ago.

Transhumance The practice of moving grazing herds between two places with different climates (e.g. from mountain to valley pastures).